*Native North Americans call trees "our standing brothers and sisters".
Humans and trees share an upright, vertical orientation.
We walk, they stand. We move and change,
they remain the quiet center of being.*

– from The Meaning of Trees by Fred Hageneder

This book is available for purchase through Createspace, Amazon.com or Ingram, or Baker and Taylor. You can also contact the author at jeaninesemon@gmail.com. Prints from this book are available through the author. The order of images were provided by Richard Jerome Bennett. Tiffany Brandt of Eye4Graphics produced the graphics and image combinations.

The Sacred Grove

JEANINE SEMON

with poetry by

ELLEN KORT

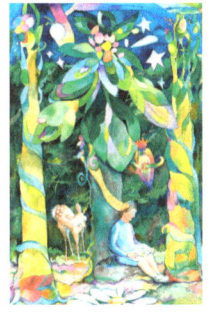

For Kris Kort and his love for writing

Ellen Kort

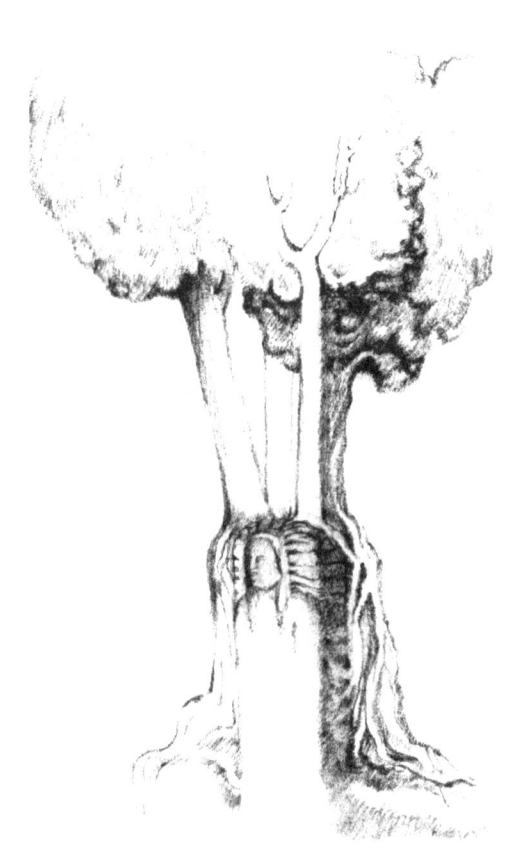

Artist's Introduction

My tree art has become more and more abstract, away from realism. I paint trees as I feel they are, homes for creatures and spirits, resting places in the summer heat, rooting the soil and holding the precious rain. Trees give comfort and health to the world.

The sketch, Indian in a Tree, came to me in my first college drawing class. It was a pivotal moment and the beginning of a lifetime of painting trees. I believe the Indian figure is my mentor.

Ellen Kort's poetry is deeply connected to my trees. An amazing partner, she writes the way I paint.

Jeanine Semon

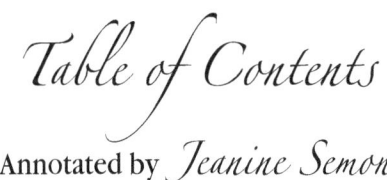

Table of Contents

Annotated by *Jeanine Semon*

To get the most out of this book, first view the images with their accompanying poetry. Secondly go through the table of contents (which is Jeanine's writing), which tells the artist's inspiration and experience painting by painting.

Hierarchy, an oil painting, came to me after a trip to a spiritual health-giving "monastery" in Brazil. Every day our teacher lectured on the special health and spiritual power in the monastery land, claiming there was a connection between their location and the "above", which watched over our planet, Earth. These people had unusual knowledge and spoke from many interesting ideas. "Hierarchy" connects to their information.

In the painting there is a flow of layers forming a large tree shape much like the Frenchman, Mondrian's early work connecting the "above" to the below, the sky to the land, accenting the horizontal and vertical plains. At the top is an important triangle in which a great haloed figure resides, with small supporting figures alongside. Cubicles of many houses flank the sides with Angel birds hovering at the peak. To me it is a close fit to the ideas flowing from the unusual Brazilian location. Subject matter lies all around us, gets into us and pops out in our creative work.

The colored drawing is of Mother Tree, which is old, hollow and large. My friends, four of us, came to the woods around Mother Tree to meditate. The area had a mystical and magical atmosphere, which appealed to the spiritual in my friends, who many times in their lives had had mystical experiences. Full of fun we decided to stand as sisters inside the beautiful tree. Later I painted a series of our experiences, the original drawing showing layers of auras expanding into the sky. The opening in the tree has since collapsed, I have contact with only one of the women, the other two have gone their way. Yet the drawings and paintings remain.

In Two by Two, a watercolor, I began to assemble creatures and plants in pairs, shaping them into a tree. I thought of Noah and the Ark, but I'd been reading about an early female Persian rug designer. Oriental rugs and I have been in love for all my adult life. In the center of Persian rugs is often a light colored medallion. Two by Two has a pair of white flowers laid onto a light blue shape in the center. If you cover that design with your hand, you'll find the composition isn't quite as strong; it's an exciting center. The creatures, the flowers, even the twigs are in pairs. The upper branches of birds and flowers were originally an unsuccessful group of sharp-ended branches. I decided to scrub them off the paper with a sponge. I then put in leaf-petals, birds, and new branches. Wisconsin's Poet Laureate, Ellen Kort's writing about Two by Two takes place outside of Noah's ark.

THE FIRST TREE - Page 7

The First Tree is a colored drawing that expands further than this image appears. There's a horizon, together with clouds, hills, moon-shaped forms rising from below the terrain. It might be a distant planet. In its aloneness the tree is strong, unafraid in it's environment.

FOUR WOMEN IN A TREE - Page 9

Picture an oil painting with four women standing in Mother Tree, described above. When I made the drawing, intuitively, I drew the tree folding her arms around the women. Protective, she became a part of the family. There are auras streaming out in all directions from this grouping. The Spiritual Presence surrounds them.

GIRL IN A GARDEN - Page 11

I almost called this watercolor, Eden. Sometimes a painting has two names. It is a fantasy land, yet I can jump inside it, step into the woods, and peer over the girl's shoulder. She is painting, unaware, as nature creeps close. This painting proves that the artist doesn't have to be realistic, the columns and huge leaves are trees, unreal but real. The starry sky floats between the trees, because I painted them that way. My art combines the web of life, the interconnectedness of all, through my individual creativity. Notice the golden stripe from the tree to the girl's head. In painting there are surprises we don't notice until afterward. Girl In A Garden is probably my most popular image.

WHITE TREE - Page 13

White Tree, an oil painting, has caused a lot of interest. It was purchased by a friend who was married to an artist, for her sister. I photographed it in the frame after she had hung it in her home. When I paint something that seems a little strange, I go through a period of not knowing whether I like it, and I wonder whether anyone else will. White Tree was like that. Yet, the longer I have the image with me, which is now in prints, the more response I get. I suppose all of my work is a little strange, certainly not like others' art. But isn't that the individual we are? White Tree is a very spiritual painting, clearly a representation of the "other side". I love it.

MUSIC TREE - Page 15

Music Tree, a watercolor, was painted for my son-in-law Jeffrey, a musician, for a CD cover. He is a pianist, and is interested in Jewish mysticism, hence the Kabbalistic Tree of Life. The drawing was swirling from the time I started the image. A network of interwoven lines, eventually I had to stop swirling and put some paint on the paper. It is flowing in harmony, a dance.

FAMILY IN THE EARTH - Page 17

Family In The Earth, a colored drawing, is part of a series of drawings about my family. I painted them nude, the natural approach to our Earth connection. They belong, we all belong to the Earth. We didn't emerge with clothes, we are brothers and sisters to all the creatures. This family lives in the Earth, content with each other. My three children, my husband, and I sit with our companion dogs. The tree is calm, happy, and protective, enjoying the setting of peace.

FAMILY IN THE TREE - Page 19

Family In The Tree is a watercolor and charcoal art image, a favorite of my viewers. Spirits, people, creatures, and stars live in the tree. The inner family occupies the central space, but Mr. Owl tops them all. Dolphins are usually in my art and here they are, floating in the branches, looking quite normal. It surprises me when viewers positively identify these inner figures as the Holy Family. Images that come to us intuitively are open-minded. The original Family In A Tree was damaged, but after days of disappointment I painted a second one from the first. To my relief it is better than the first.

MAGIC TREE - Page 21

A watercolor, Magic Tree bends the rules flowing in the swirls of the Universe. The tree is not solid; it vibrates with energy, holding the jumping off place for the large green tree frog who is in its dance, unafraid of leaving the tree. The dolphin and red bird are moving in this cosmic stream, a flowing river.

LOVE COUPLE AND BEYOND - Page 23

This Love Couple comes from my series of family drawings, which grow from the DNA of the Universe. My nudes illustrate the natural interconnection of life, growth, and plants. Their inertia moves the world forward from remembering the past. The tree is alive, holds it all, understands all.

UNITY TREE - Page 25

Unity Tree, an oil painting, is similar to Family In A Tree, but shows its inner and outer vibrations. It is filled with birds, dolphins, and stars and above is a large encompassing spirit figure. Mr. Owl watches it all. The name, Unity, says everything; none of us stands alone, life works better when we have partners, as God tells us, "Seek a mate, make a family, have friends, work together." The limited palette adds to the unity.

NIGHT WALK Page 27

Done in watercolor, Night Walk expresses the feelings I had over twenty-nine years of walking dogs with my husband, down the river path behind our home in Menomonee Falls, Wisconsin. In the dark evenings, feeling the summer breeze, knowing the short loyal years of our animals, I had a keen awareness of the brevity of life, our own mortality. The path beneath our feet, the sound of the river, the trees we watched from their early planting stayed with us for years. This painting is abstract, the figures revealed along with a little creature curled up in the foliage. There is a shadow-like man, another dog above him, and a moon in the trees. Since my art is without planning, there are surprises that push themselves into the painting, that belong.

RIVER WALK Page 29

Here it is, the final painting in this little book, River Walk, an oil painting done in my younger years. When you paint what you love in the outdoors, occasionally a person comes along, or a dog. If you quick grab the image where you see it, in the same technique as the painting, don't spend too much time on it, you'll get an extra piece of life that enhances the painting. Afterword, you can't envision the painting without it. This boy is our neighbor. The dog is our first Sheltie, Chipper, a special dog, who only lived seven years. On this riverbank I spent many hours sitting on a camp stool with my watercolors on my lap, painting that scene, the stone bridge, my husband's family business, an old mill building alongside the river, transformed into a small town department store. My husband, our dogs and our children would visit me and the classes I taught in the summer. It's hard to believe I don't do that anymore. But I do paint, most every day, loving it more and more, grateful that I am an artist.

Hierarchy

The mystics say the world was built
layer upon layer by great spirit
beings rising from the fertile
green earth   reaching for the open
sky   for the outstretched hands
of wisdom keepers from another
realm   Listen   Together they know
every measure of grace and wonder
Look   together they have created
a hierarchy of love and peace

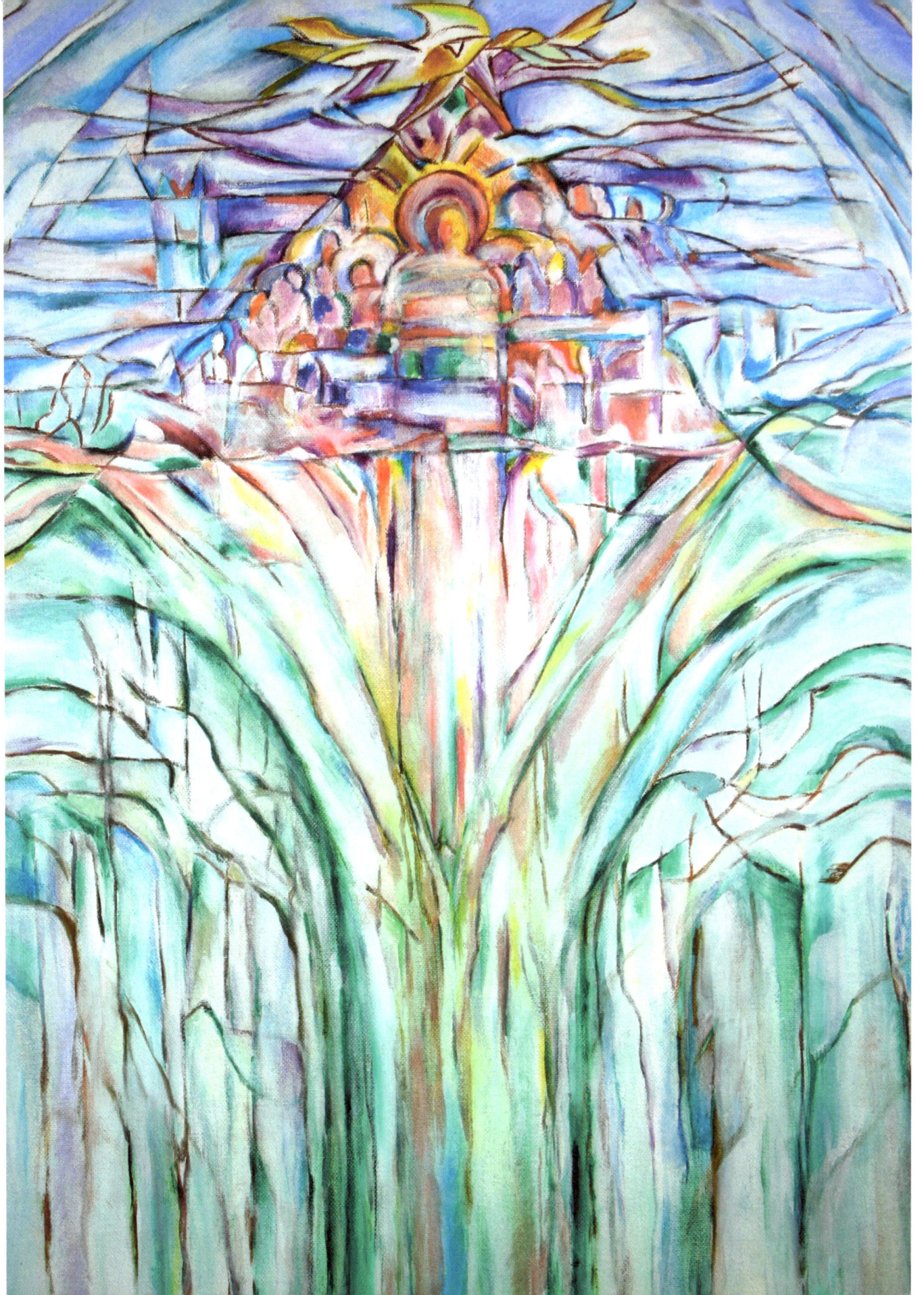

Mother Tree

In the first story of the world
the mother womb of the tree opened
Her blood roots   a long time
in the earth became a slow warming
of green   Her arms welcomed the sun
gave witness to the moon   Is it any
wonder we can hear the leaves
singing   The whisper of our names
browse in the wind   tremble the air
still cling to the soft meat of her heart

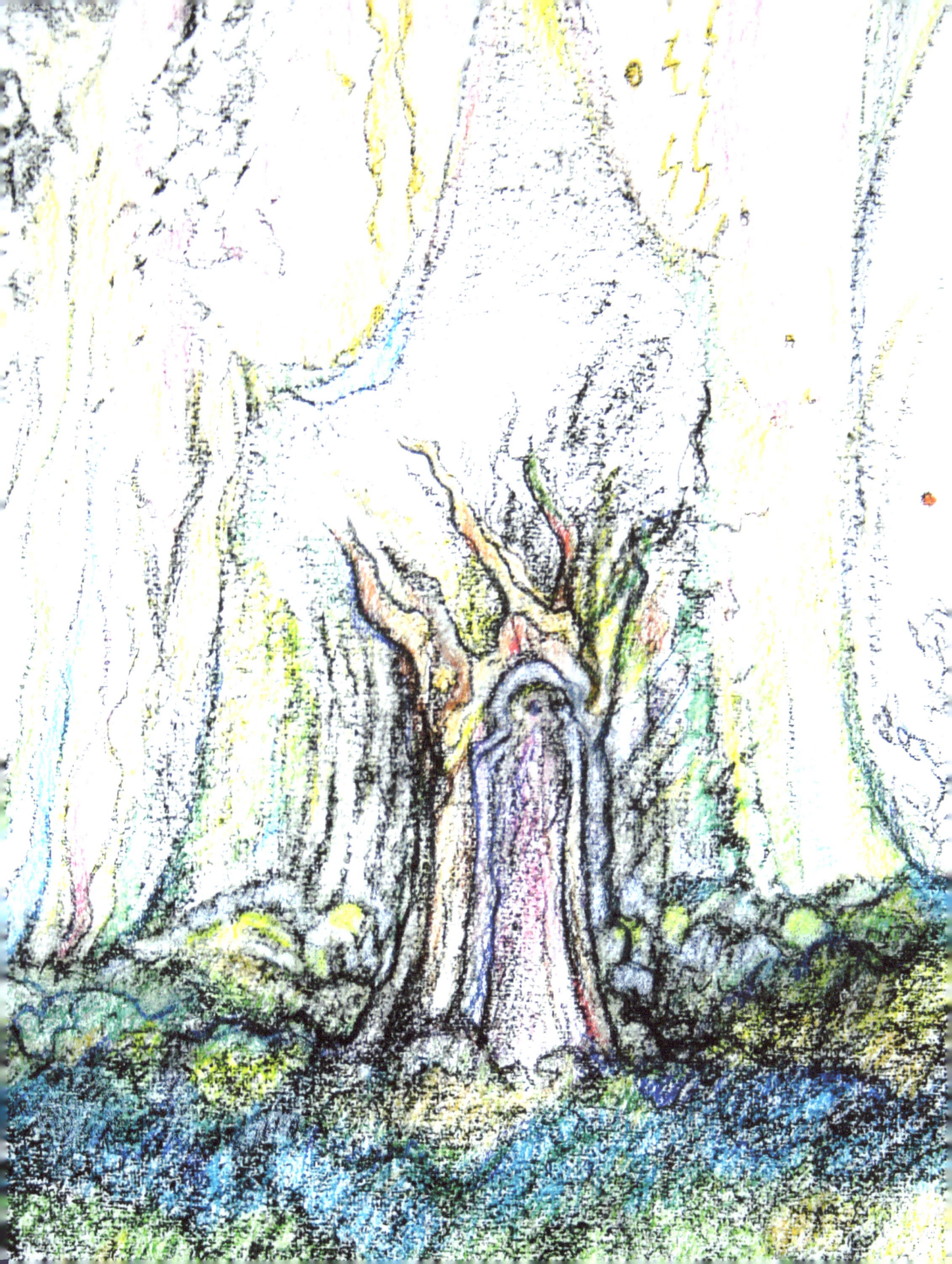

Two By Two

The animals came one by one
two by two long before Noah
knew their names   long before
we knew how to trace
the bloodlines that cling
to the heart   every breath
that marks the air   each of us
made of skin and bones
each of us a collaborator
between earth and sky
the tree of life balanced
on the back of the world

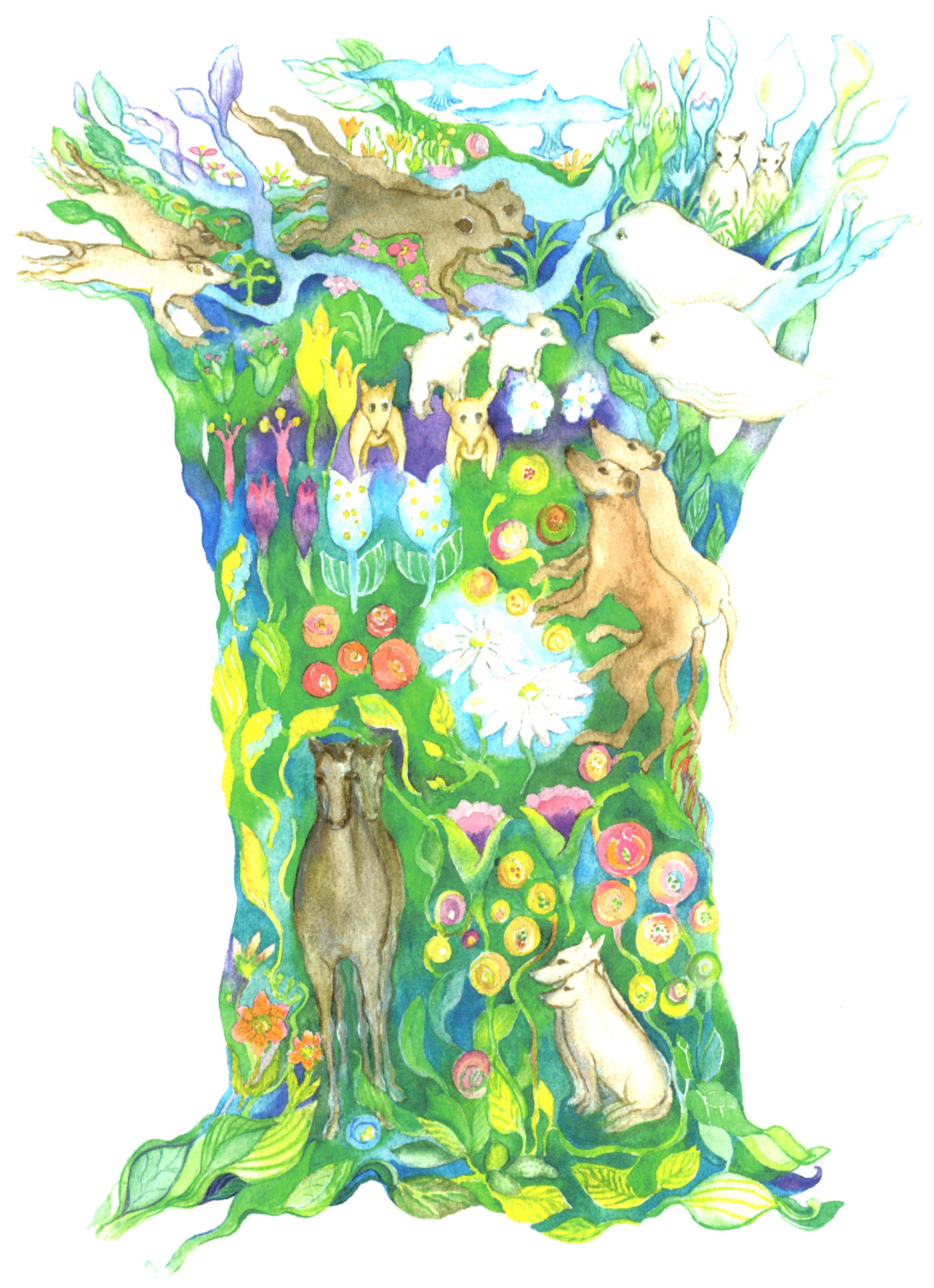

The First Tree

When Mother Earth brought forth
the very first tree   she saw it
as womankind   feminine spirit
light bringer   a gift to the new
world   And when the tree unfolded
its branches and lifted them
to the sky   the sun rose in welcome

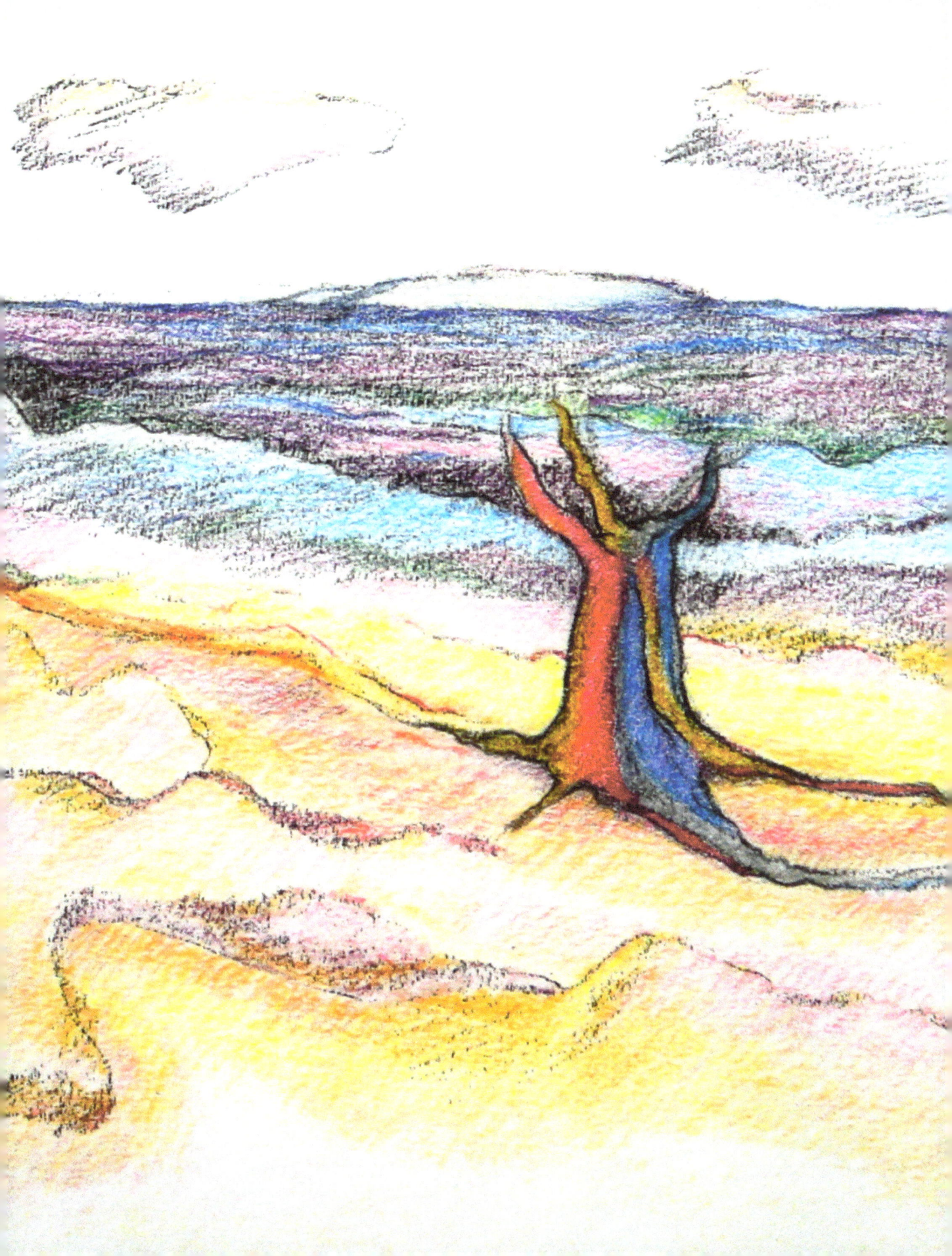

Four Women In A Tree

Kneel at the heartwood of the tree
lay down charms for daughter   mother
grandmother   great grandmother
light candles   an offering of small
flames for the blessing of their names
for women who love the silken rasp
of wind   who trust the outstretched
wings of owl   women of wisdom
a circle of women holding one another

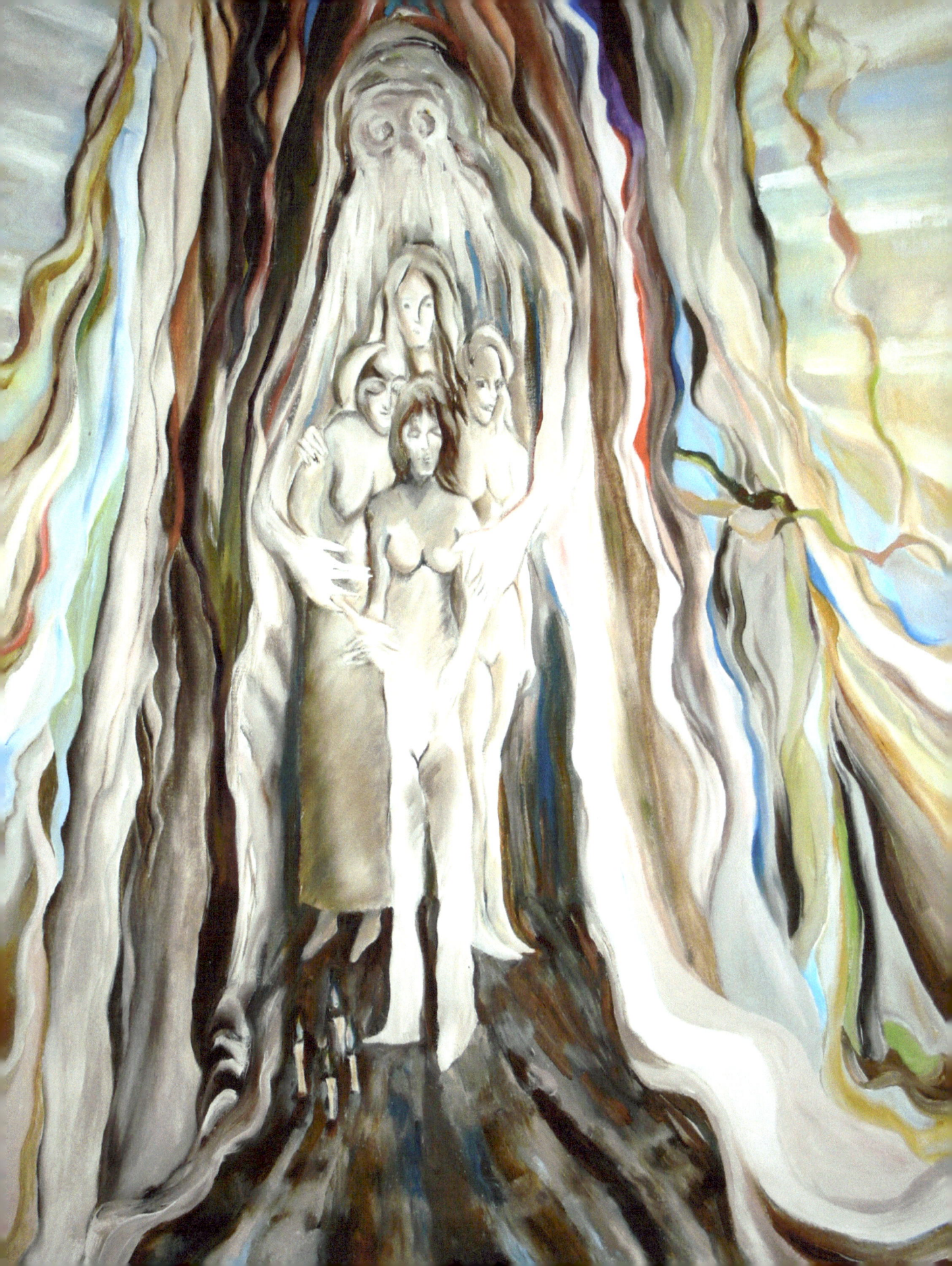

Girl In A Garden

She discovered the garden
on an early morning walk
such a magical place   such an
exuberance of light   She could
feel all the boisterous colors
well up inside her and knew
she had to bring canvas and paints
and brushes   She settled in
against a tree   could smell red
and yellow   could hear
the sound of purple   Who can
explain how the hand moves
of its own accord   follows
the stirring in the heart   lays open
the daydream folds of memory

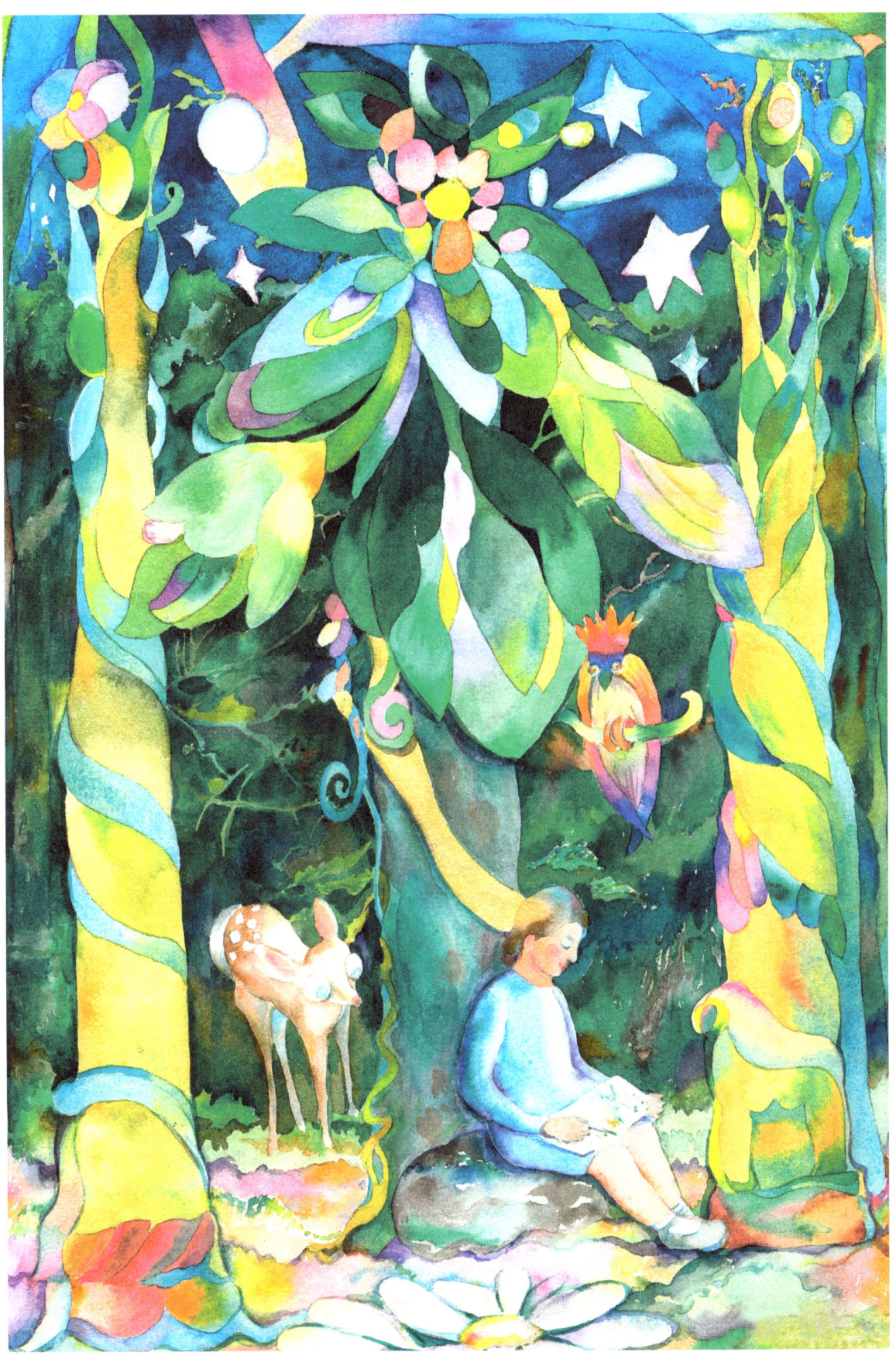

White Tree

Light is an endless migration
a repetition   a reverence
And love is the way we gather it in
Ask the small deer seeking shelter
in the shadow of the white tree
the buck who watches near by
Ask the flying fish   weaving in
and out of their element   the wolf
who lies down in front of the man
both already knowing that trust
is the hardest kind of love
And isn't it our job to love the light
to walk in it's everlasting radiance

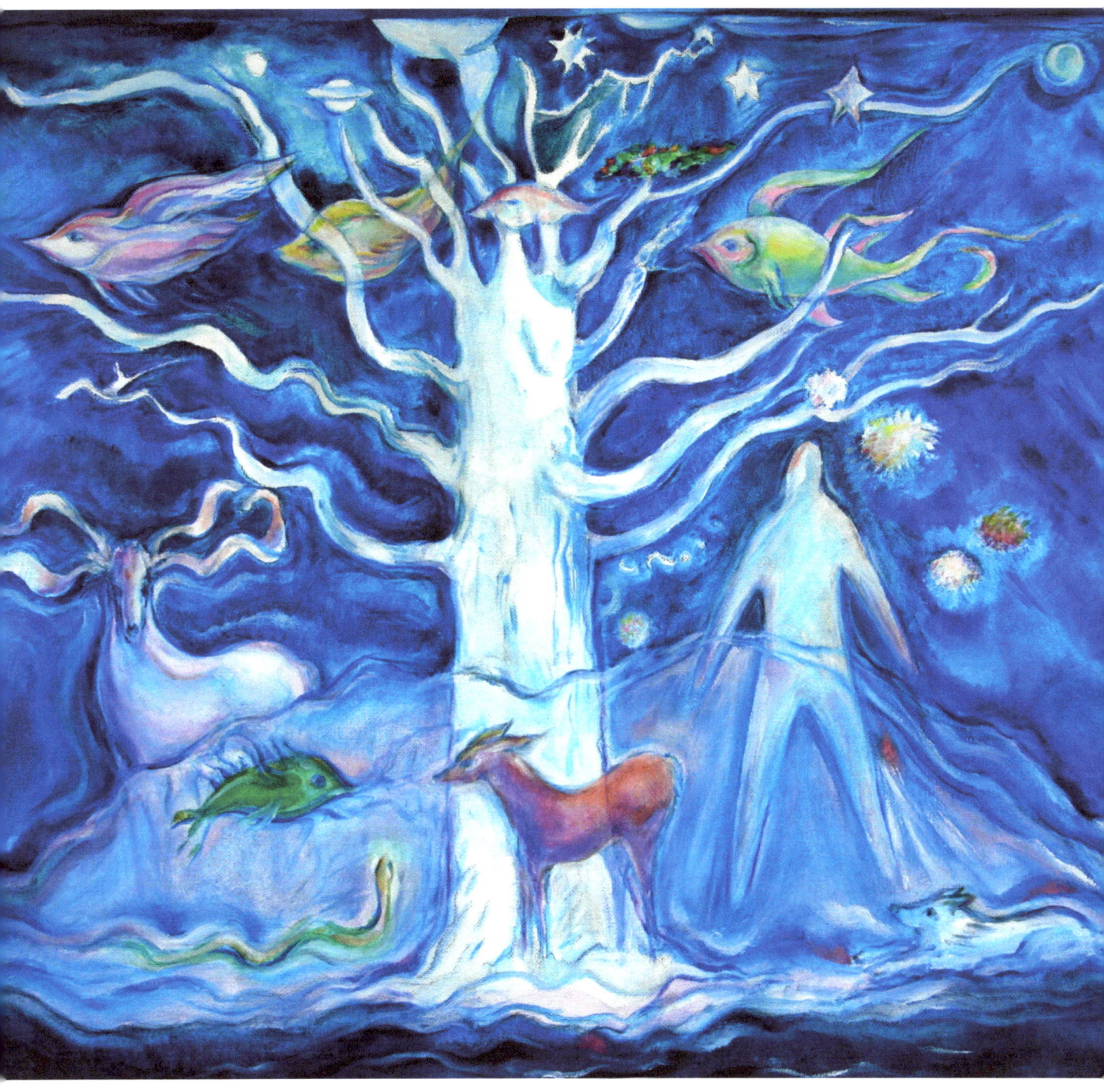

Music Tree

The tree opened its arms
and the music came   the soft
brush of a great vision carried
by unseen currents of air
a red path of sunrise etched
against lavender blue sky
The sing song strands of music
flowing like a river   its liquid
weave   one beautiful turn
after another   its echo rising
and falling   catching the wind
the open hunger of our heart

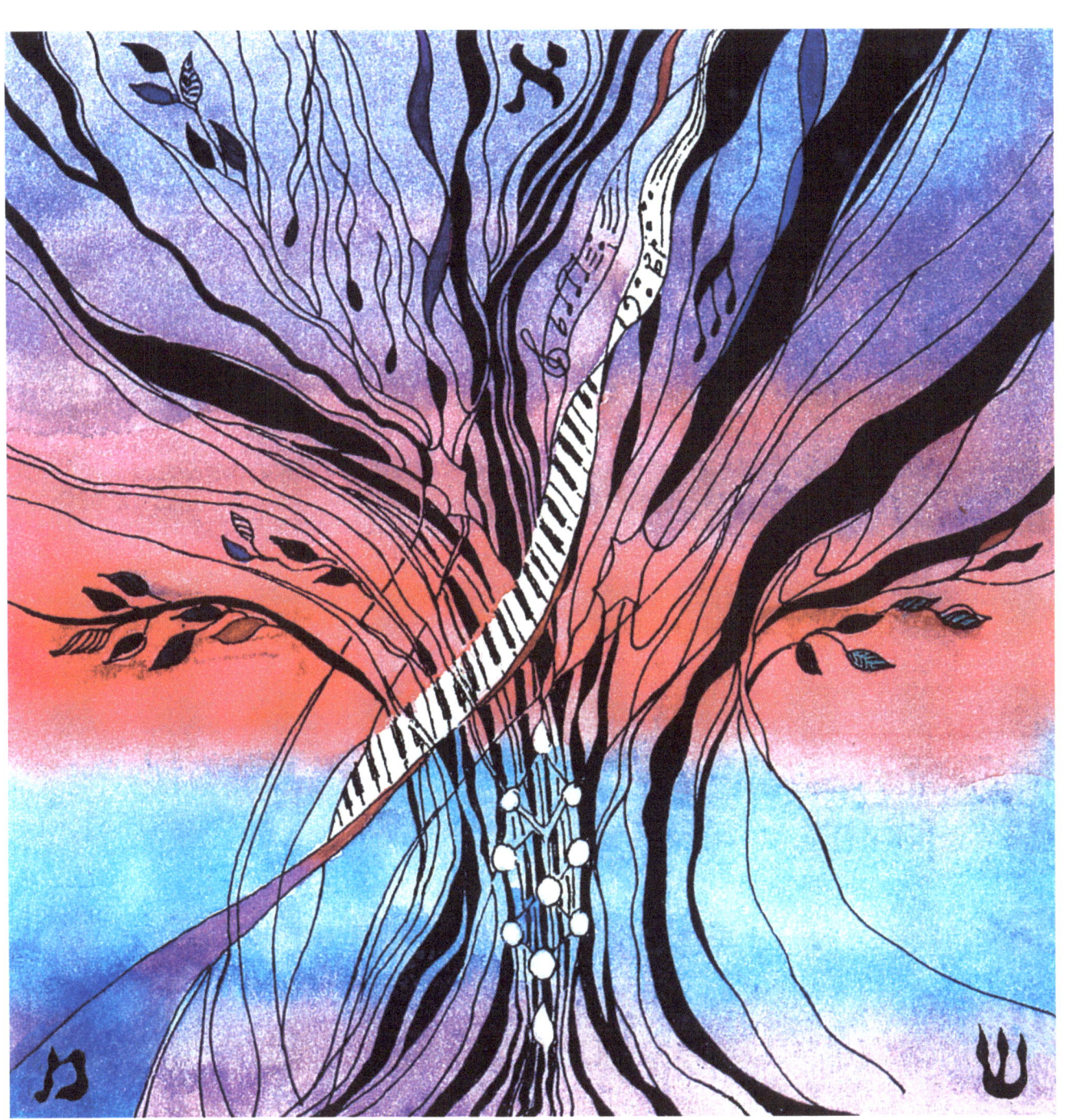

Family in the Earth

Mother Earth named them
one by one as the fertile roots
of every living thing   She called
them threshold of light
first flesh of trees   She called
them throat singers   hummers
sweepers of shadowed grass
She called them up and out
of the darkness   lifted them
toward the sun   She called them
and called them and they came

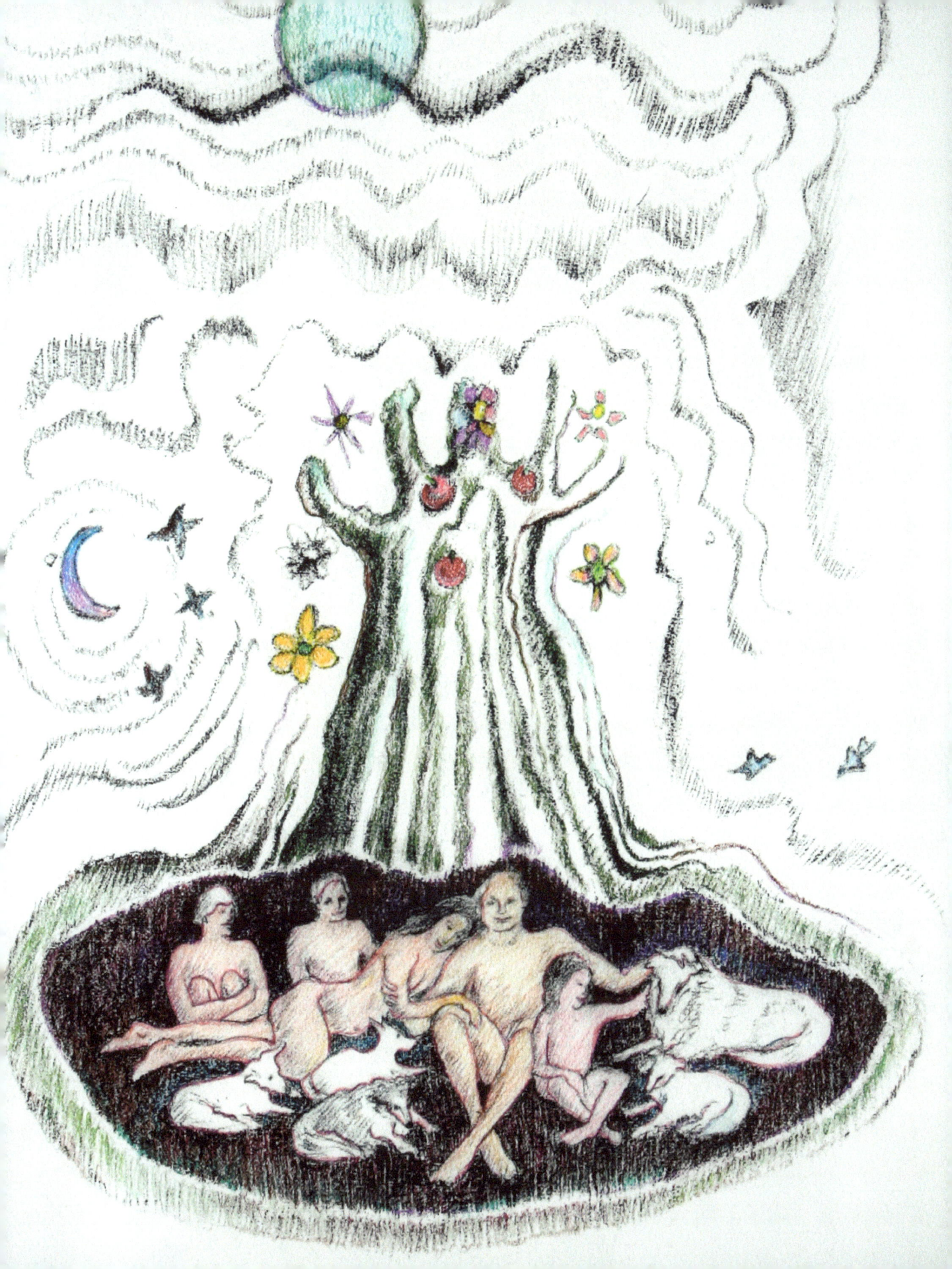

Family in a Tree

This tree   a living body
of all that is holy in the universe
the common narrative of owls
joyful vibrations of dolphins
unbridled bird songs   each one
a small prayer   that fattens
the wind   and each of us a small
point of light resting in the belly
of the tree   an everlasting thread
of those who came before us

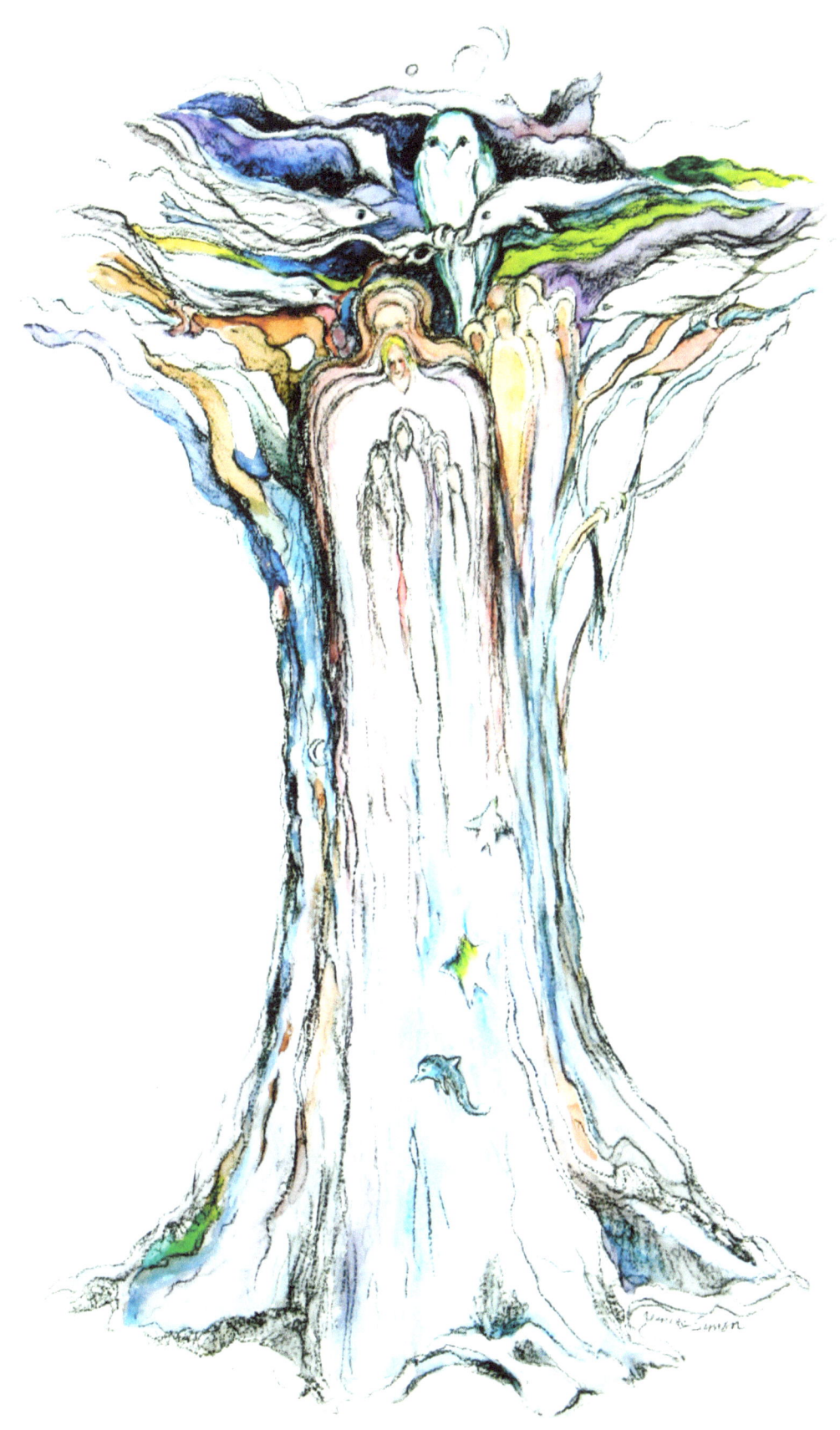

Magic Tree

A red bird takes to the air
and carries its color with it
a streak of glory   and offers it
to the tree   A dolphin swims
up river   The tree opens
its welcoming arms
and the dolphin swims through
the blue-red water of life
A tree frog   quietly dreaming
discovers it can fly
and as the world pulses around
them   they find a new order
a connectedness called joy

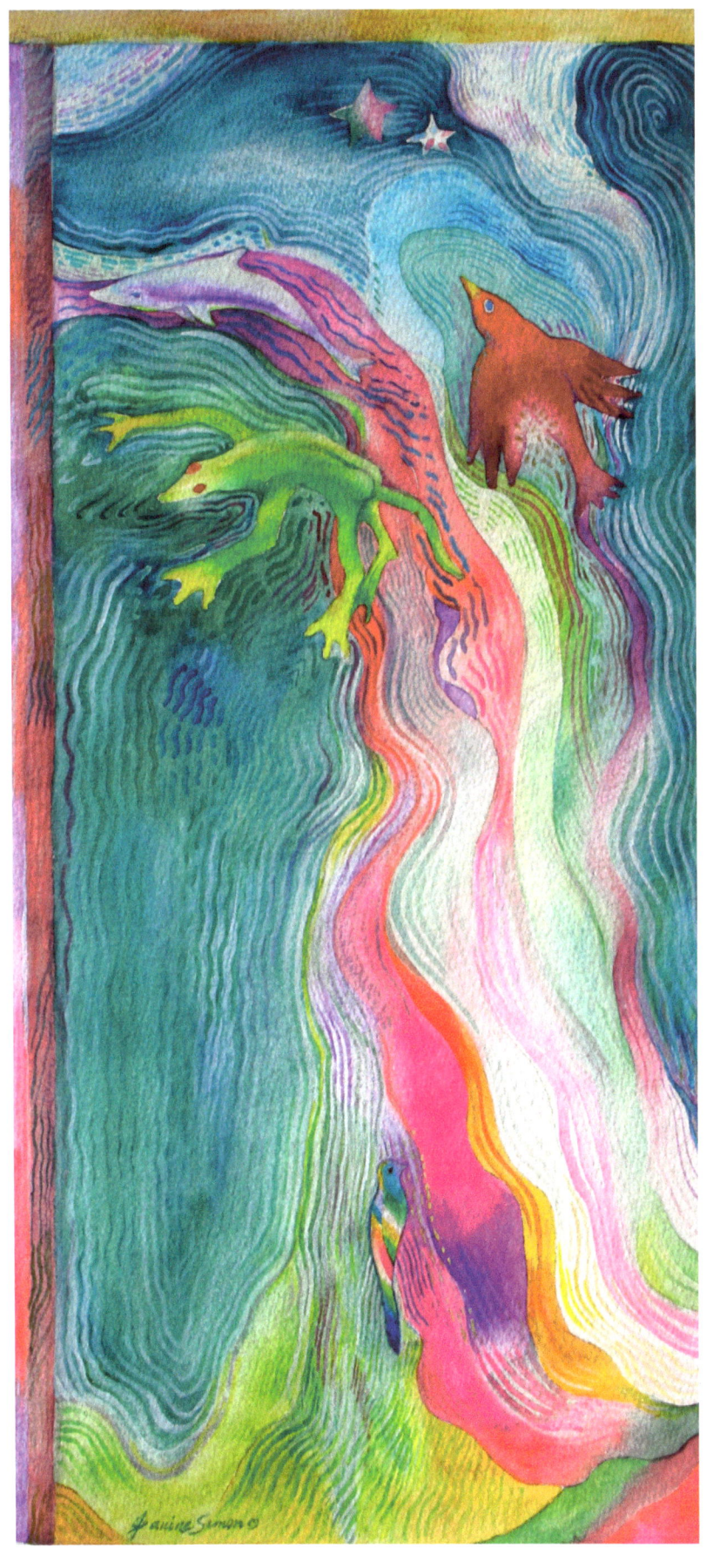

Love Couple and Beyond

Bless the woman and man
the original love force
of the world   their lives
indelibly etched by those
who came before them
Bless the man and woman
who keep the world spinning
on its axis   knowing how
time moves the distant horizon
closer   There is an everyday
rhythm to their love   to be
spoken by those who follow
Their life story told over and over
by those who remember

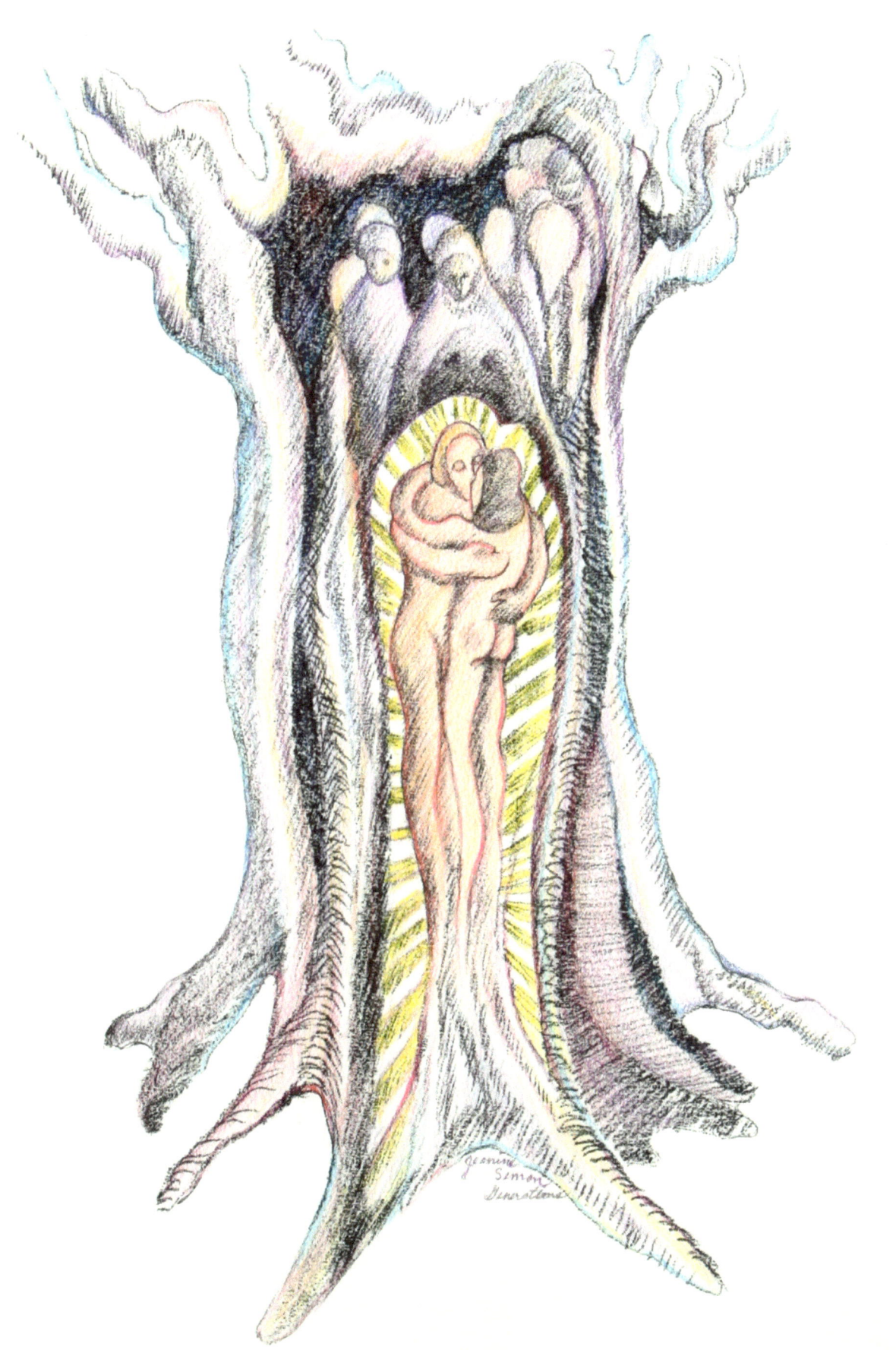

Unity Tree

Let us circle the tree   let it
rise   Bless the strength
of its roots   its wings of song
the way it wears the stunning
light of morning   Let it be
a lamp for peace   a prayer wheel
where love circles and multiplies
Let it be an altar   a resting place
where we can tell one another
all the stories of the world

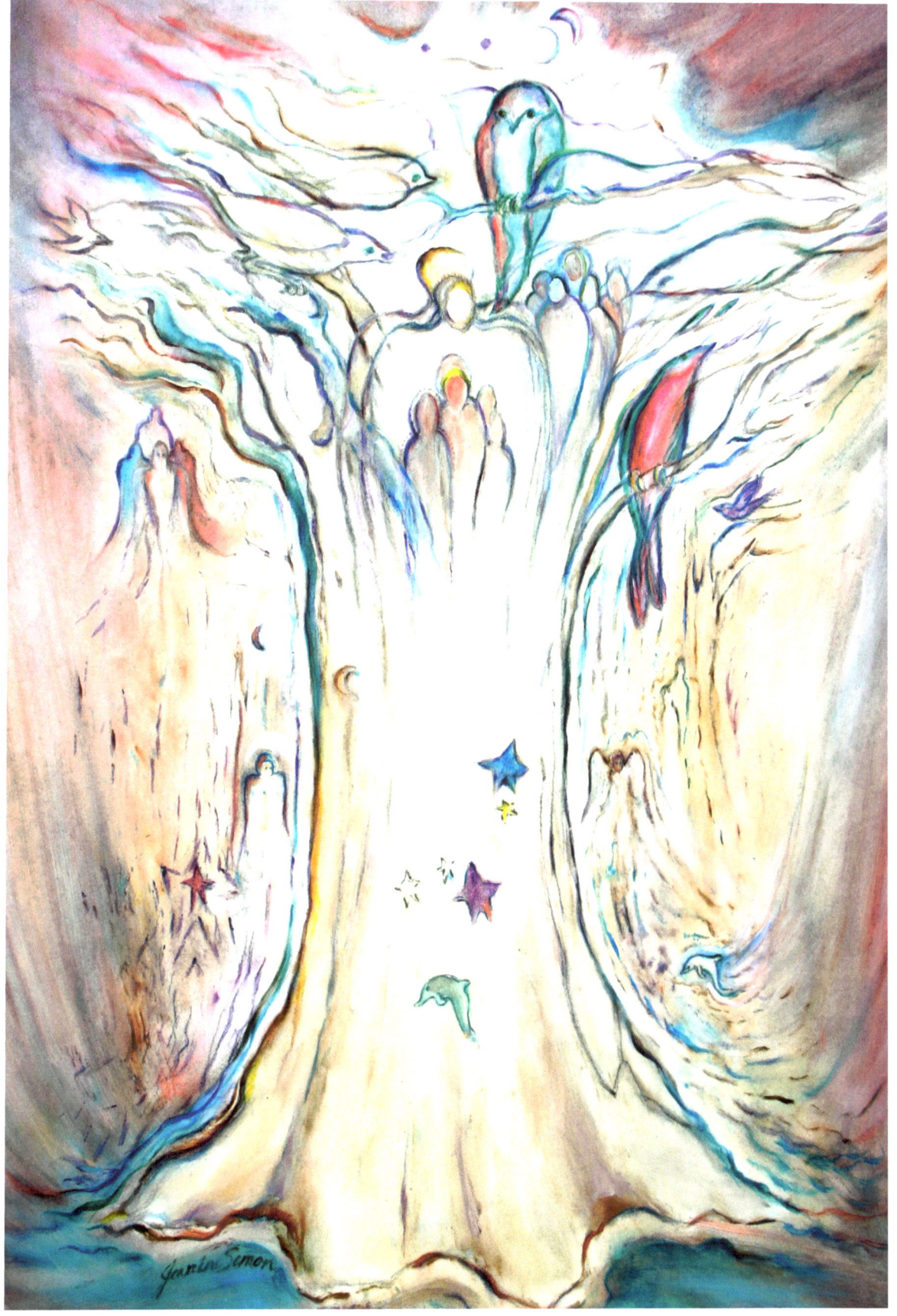

Night Walk

Late at night when the moon
is awake   when trees bloom
into giant orbs of blues
and greens   we put on our
night robes   walk the path
by the river   paint pots
in our pockets   carry our
paint brushes like walking sticks
We paint in the dark   breathe in
the insistent hum of stars
shifting clouds   the night silence
broken now and then by the cry
of a small creature we cannot
name   by the faint murmur of birds

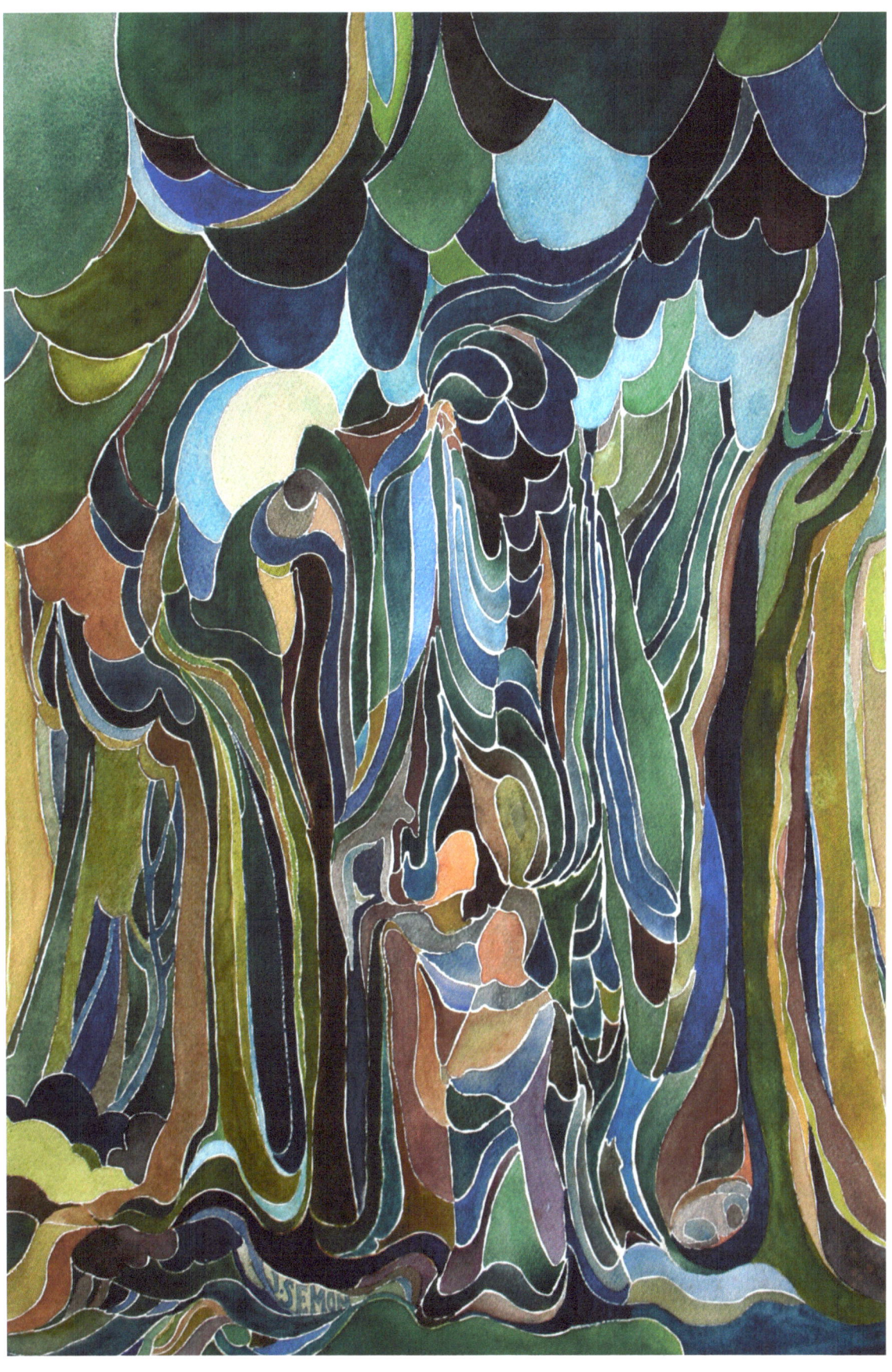

River Walk

It is a perfect day for a boy
and his dog to go walking
The path stretches ahead
as though it might take them
to the edge of the earth
The boy loves the way the sun
lays shadows across the ground
He names the trees   listens for
the chirping of crickets
and the dog pays close attention
These two   traveling companions
These two   owning the world

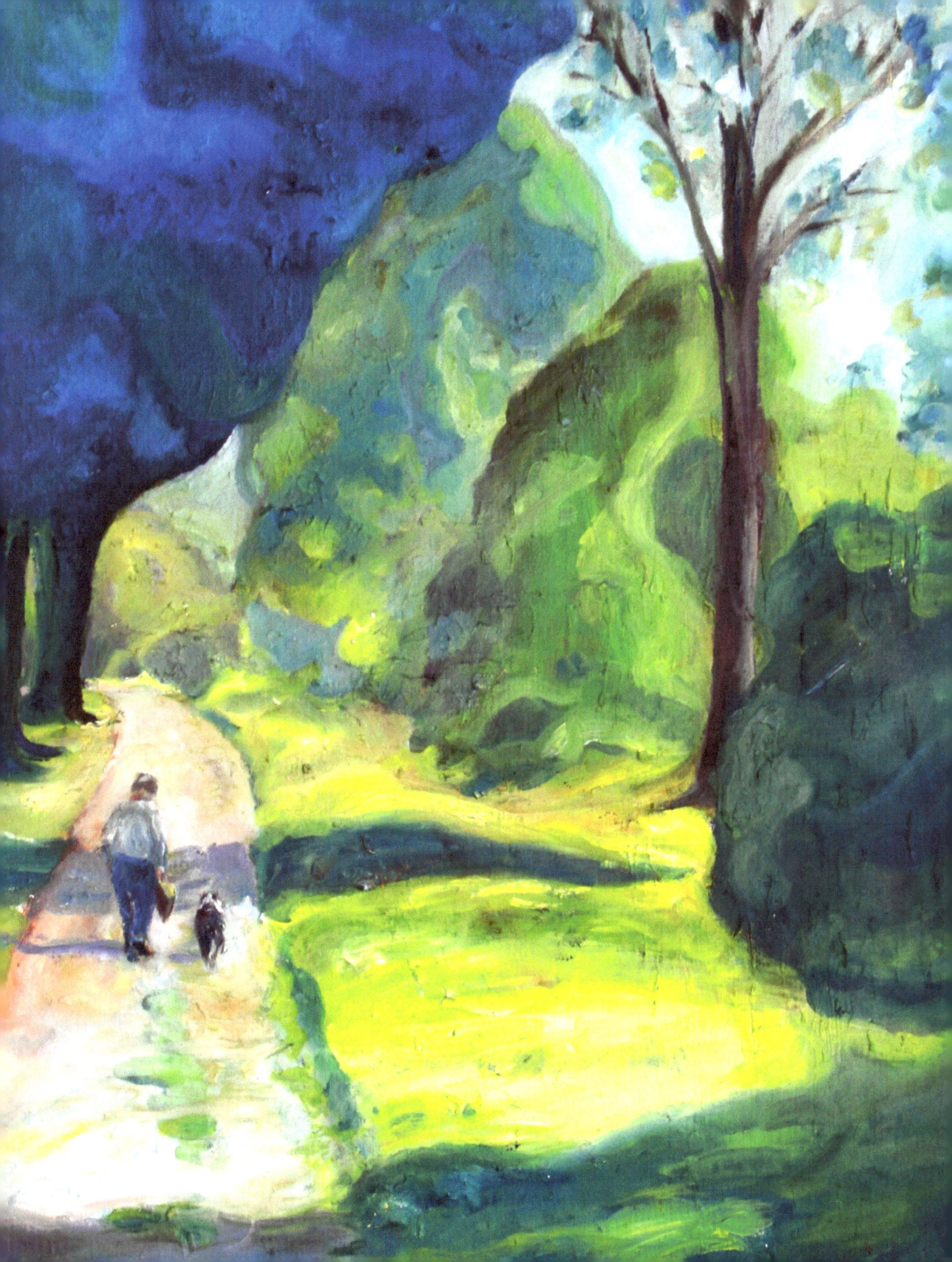

Biography

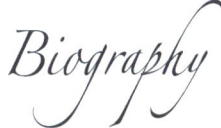

JEANINE SEMON (pictured right)

The artist in JEANINE SEMON was declared by age eight, but the attainment came about circuitously through marriage and child-raising. Her early painting took place on the Wisconsin landscape. Jeanine later made her way to the University of Wisconsin and into a love of primitive arts with its respect for the power of nature. Subject matter combining all life arose from her intuitive, which continues today. Jeanine and her husband Ed walk and swim in the northwoods of Wisconsin, making their home in Lac du Flambeau, both growing in painting and writing. Jeanine believes art is in the DNA and is there for everyone. "It makes us happy and heals us."

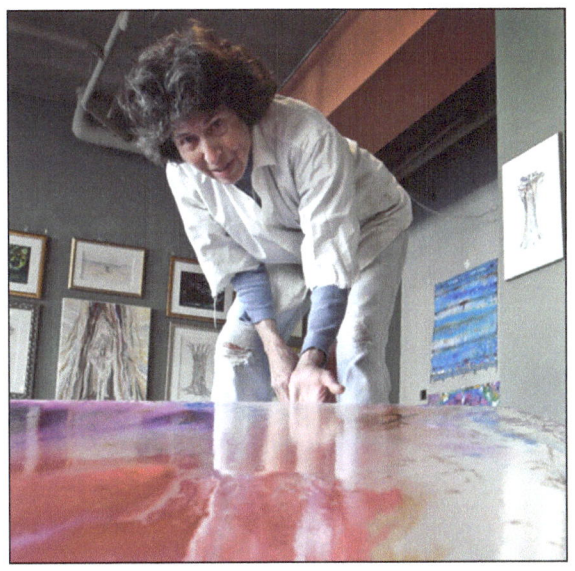

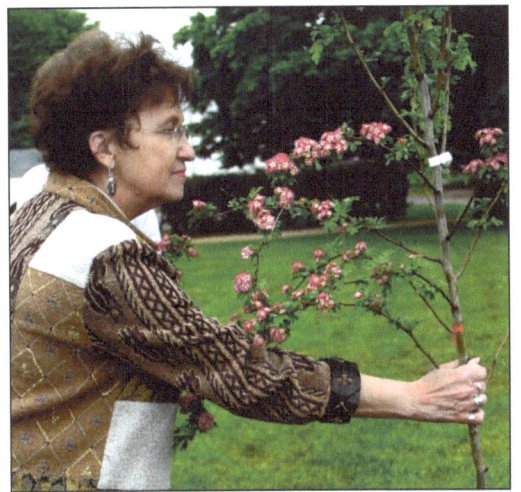

ELLEN KORT is Wisconsin's first Poet Laureate. She is teacher, mother, and pride of Appleton, Wisconsin. Her poetry is universally sought after, most recently added to a botanical garden sculpture, and the motivating poetry for a Green Bay symphony orchestra performance. Her poetry teaching has found its way into the hearts of students, children and adults. Known for her humanity, students remark, "When I was in Ellen's class I became a poet."

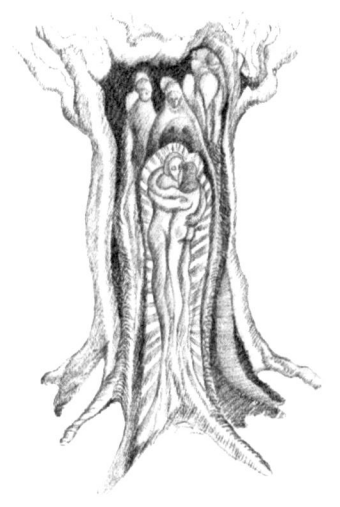